LEVEL 1

Frogs

Elizabeth Carney

NATIONAL GEOGRAPHIC

Washington, D.C.

For my parents, Marty and Cindy Carney, who charitably endured my collections of slimy creatures. —E. C.

Library of Congress Cataloging-in-Publication Data
Carney, Elizabeth, 1981-
Frogs! / by Elizabeth Carney.
p. cm. -- (National Geographic readers)
ISBN 978-1-4263-0392-0 (pbk. : alk. paper) -- ISBN 978-1-4263-0393-7 (hardcover : alk. paper)
1. Frogs--Juvenile literature. I. Title.
QL668.E2C346 2009
597.8'9--dc22
2008014028l

Front Cover: © Digital Vision; 1, 14 (bottom), 27 (top): © Shutterstock; 2: © Michael and Patricia Fogden/CORBIS; 4-5: © Michael Durham/Minden Pictures/Getty Images; 6 (left): © Roger Wilmshurst/Frank Lane Picture Agency/CORBIS; 6 (right): © Pete Oxford/Minden Pictures/Getty Images; 7 (left): © Joe McDonald/CORBIS; 7 (right), 32 (bottom, left): © Gallo Images/CORBIS; 8, 32 (top, left): © Norbert Wu/Science Faction/Getty Images; 9: © Gerald Lopez/Associated Press; 10, 17: © Mark Moffett/Minden Pictures/Getty Images; 12: © Visuals Unlimited/CORBIS; 13 (top), 21 (top): © Pete Oxford/Nature Picture Library; 13 (bottom): © Photos.com/Jupiter Images; 14-15: © Buddy Mays/CORBIS; 16: © Steve Winter/National Geographic/Getty Images; 18 (top), 26 (bottom), 30 (bottom): © Michael and Patricia Fogden/Minden Pictures/Getty Images; 18 (bottom): © Michael Lustbader/drr.net; 19 (top), 24: © Christian Ziegler/Danita Delimont Agency/drr.net; 19 (bottom): © Digital Vision; 20: © Liquidlibrary/Jupiter Images; 21 (bottom): © Wegner/ARCO/Nature Picture Library; 22-23: © Glow Images/Alamy; 25: © Robert Clay/California Stock Photo/drr.net; 26 (top), 32 (top, right): © Paula Gallon; 27 (bottom): © Carol Wien/Mira; 28: © Don Farrall/Photodisc/Getty Images; 29: Geoff Brightling/Dorling Kindersley/Getty Images; 30 (top): © Geoff Brightling/Dorling Kindersley/DK Images; 31 (top, both): © Joel Sartore/drr.net; 31 (bottom): © David A. Northcott/CORBIS; 32 (bottom, right): © Sue Daly/Nature Picture Library.

Collection ISBN: 978-1-4263-1197-0

Printed in China
18/RRDS/5

Table of Contents

Splash!

Pacific Chorus Frog

Q What happened to the frog's car when it broke down?

A It got toad.

Splish, splash.
What is that sound?
What is hopping and
jumping around?
What loves to swim?
What loves to eat bugs?
It's a frog!
Can you hop like a frog?

Frogs live all over the world, except Antarctica. Frogs usually live in wet places. They like rivers, lakes, and ponds.

Antarctica is the continent at the South Pole.

Ribbit!

Habitat: The natural place where a plant or animal lives

But some frogs live in trees. Some even live in the desert. Frogs can be found all over the world. Wherever they live, that's their habitat.

Croak!

Look at this frog croaking! Some frogs' throats puff up when they make sounds. Each type of frog makes its own sound.

Lake Frog

Coqui Frog

Ribbit!

Croak: The deep, hoarse noise that a frog makes

The coqui frog is named after the sound it makes. It sounds like "CO-KEE!" This frog is the size of a quarter. Even small frogs can make loud noises.

Frogs make different sounds for different reasons. Sometimes it's to warn other frogs of danger. Sometimes it's to call to frogs nearby.

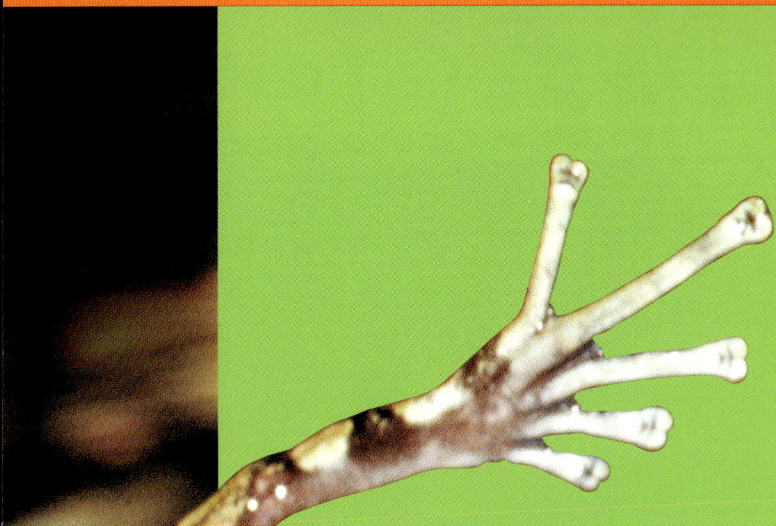

Dancing Frog

This frog lives around noisy waterfalls. Other frogs would not be able to hear its calls. So it dances instead! It sticks out one leg, and then the other. Can you dance like this frog?

Frog Food

What is a frog's favorite food? Usually it's insects. Frogs eat dragonflies and crickets and other bugs.

Green Frog

Q Why are frogs so happy?

A They eat what bugs them!

Some frogs eat bigger animals like worms and mice. The American bullfrog even eats other frogs!

What's that pink flash? It's how a frog catches bugs. It shoots out its long, sticky tongue at a passing bug. The frog pulls the bug into its mouth.

If your tongue were as long as a frog's, it would reach to your belly button!

Green Tree Frog

Every Size and Color

Frogs can be many different sizes.

The smallest frog is as big as a fingernail. The largest is as big as a rabbit.

Goliath Frog

Frogs can be different colors, too.

Some are green or brown.

Others have stripes or spots.

Frogs can be red, yellow, or orange.

They can even be bright blue!

Watch Out!

These colorful frogs may look pretty. But watch out! These frogs have poison in their skin. Their bright color warns enemies not to eat them.

Poison Dart Frog

Ribbit!

Poison:
Something that can kill or hurt living things

This little frog is only an inch long. Its name is Terribilis, which means "the terrible one." How did it get this name? By being the most deadly frog of all! One Terribilis has enough poison to kill 20,000 mice.

Q What do stylish frogs wear?

A Jumpsuits.

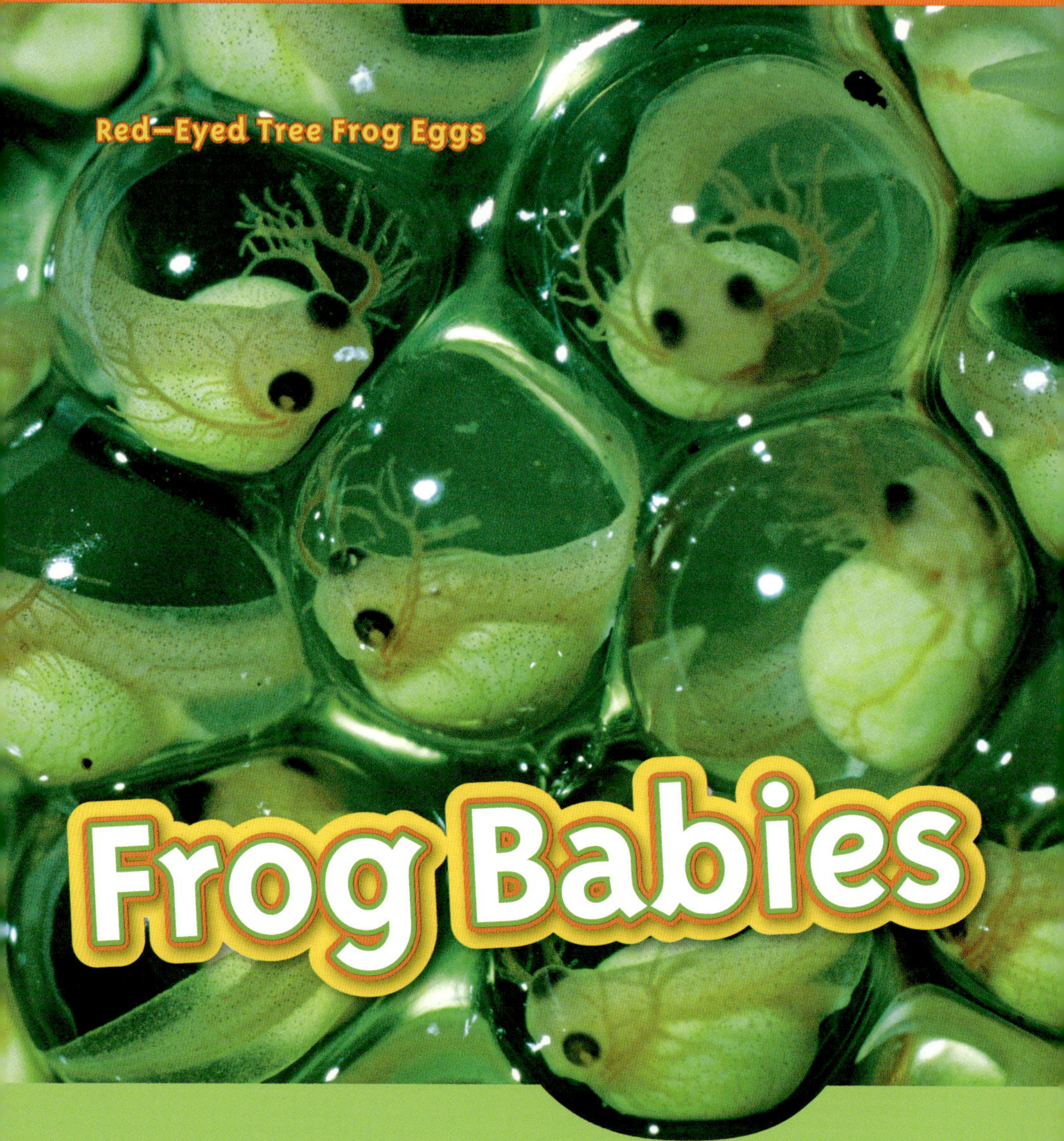

Red-Eyed Tree Frog Eggs

Frog Babies

All frogs, even the Terribilis, have mothers. Mother frogs lay eggs. When the eggs are ready, out pop the tadpoles!

Tadpoles are baby frogs. But they don't look like frogs yet. Tadpoles have tails. They live only in water.

Pacific Tree Frog Tadpole

Tadpoles grow up to be frogs.

1 At first they breathe underwater with gills.

Ribbit!

Gills: The body parts on the sides of a fish or tadpole through which it breathes

2 They grow lungs for breathing air.

3 They grow legs for hopping and swimming.

4 In three months, they lose their tails.

It's time to hop out of the water!

Toads Are Frogs, Too!

What's the difference between toads and frogs?

Toads are a type of frog. Frogs spend most of their lives around water. Toads spend more time on dry land. Their bodies are built for where they live.

SUPER FROGS!

A FAKE FACE FOOLS ENEMIES WHEN THIS FROG TURNS AROUND!

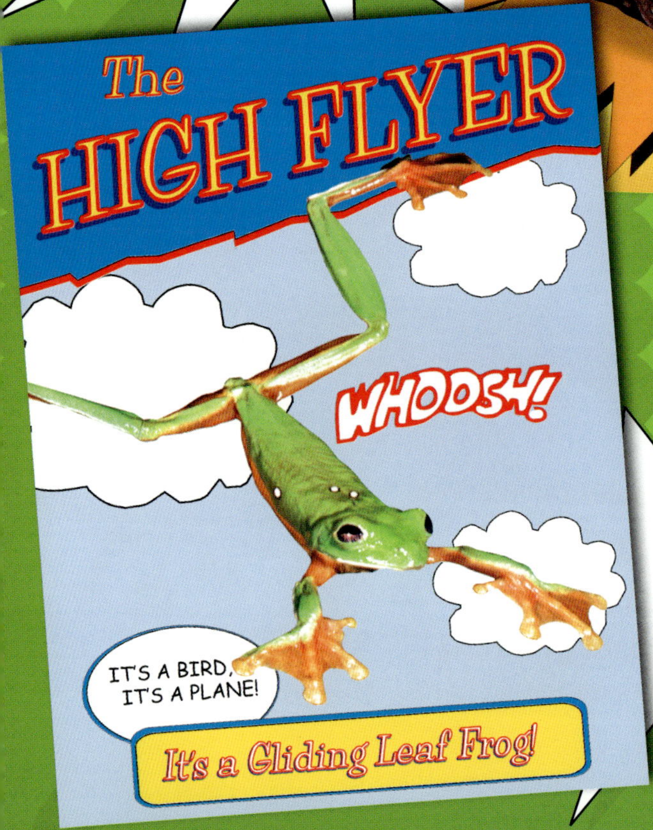

ANY FROG CAN JUMP, BUT WATCH ME GLIDE!

LOUD-MOUTHED FROG LEAVES ENEMIES STUNNED!

HE'S A MASTER OF DISGUISE!

CROAK
The deep, hoarse noise that a frog makes

GILLS
The body parts on the sides of a fish or tadpole through which it breathes

HABITAT
The natural place where a plant or animal lives

POISON
Something that can kill or hurt living things

LEVEL 1

Ants

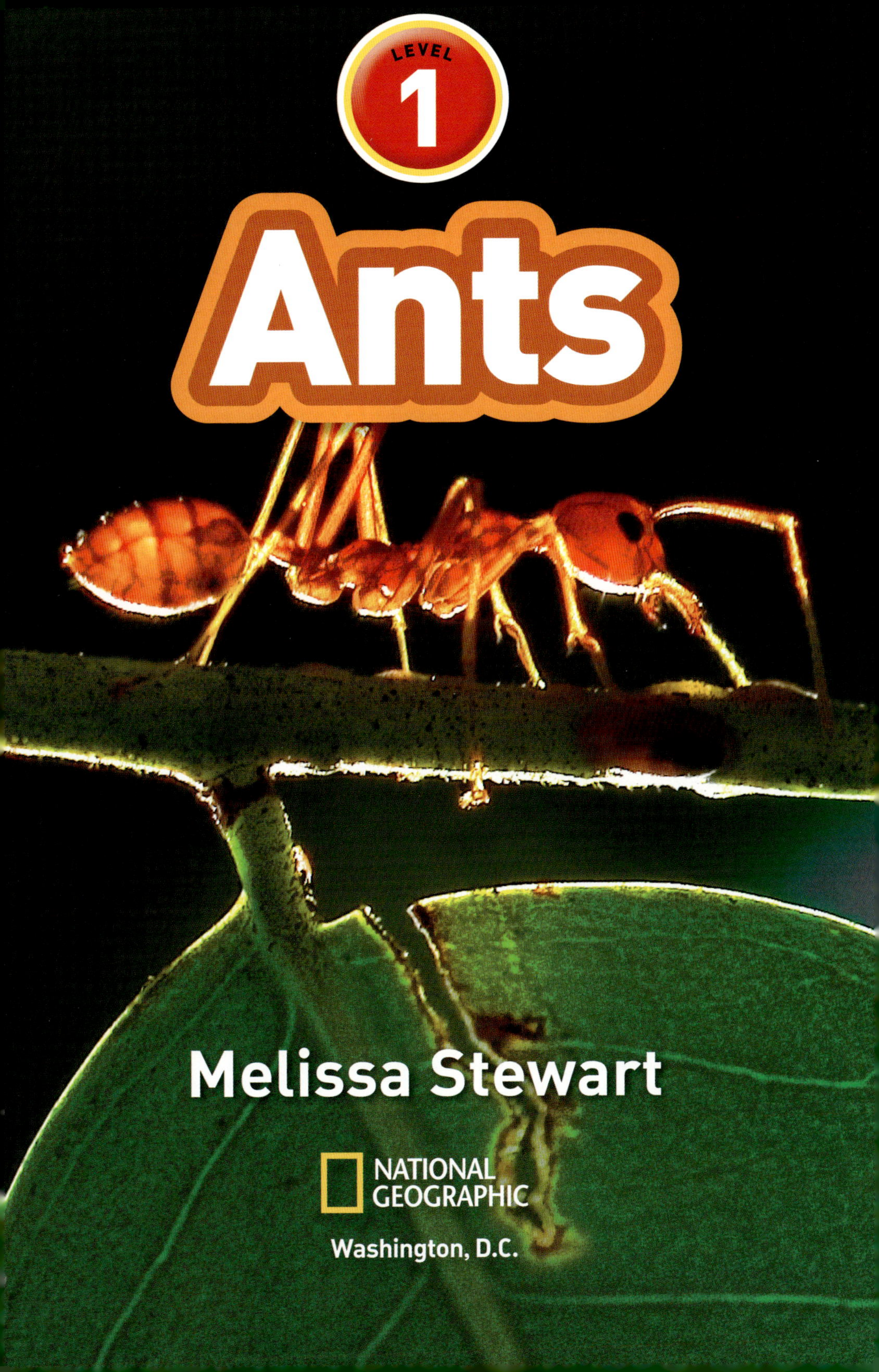

Melissa Stewart

NATIONAL GEOGRAPHIC

Washington, D.C.

For Claire, who sometimes seems to have ants in her pants. — Melissa

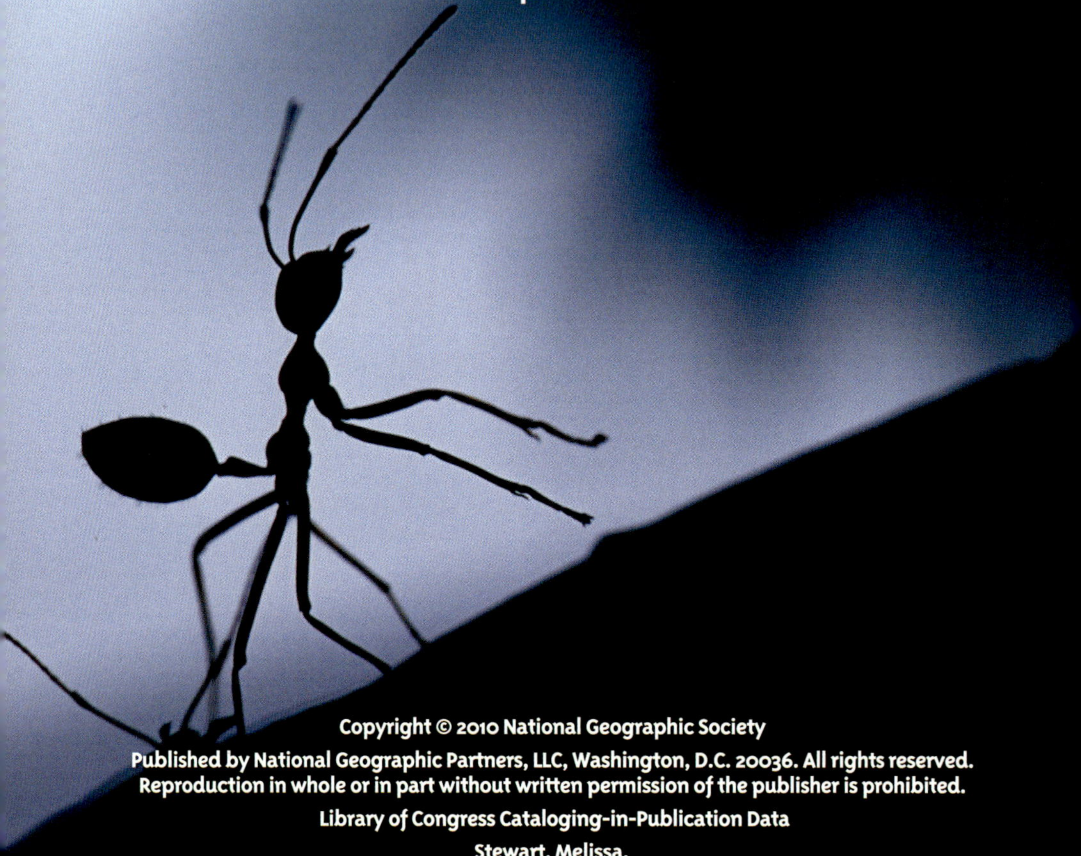

Library of Congress Cataloging-in-Publication Data

Stewart, Melissa.
Ants! / by Melissa Stewart.
p. cm.
ISBN 978-1-4263-0609-9 (library binding : alk. paper) -- ISBN 978-1-4263-0608-2 (trade pbk. : alk. paper)
1. Ants--Juvenile literature. I. Title.
QL568.F7S82 2010
595.79'6--dc22
2009035188

Cover: © George B. Diebold/Corbis; 1, 6-7, 28 (inset), 30 (inset): © Shutterstock; 2: © Jason Edwards/National Geographic/Getty Images; 4-5, 26: © Christian Ziegler/Minden Pictures/National Geographic Stock; 8, 16 (inset), 16-17, 22-23 (bottom), 23, 24 (inset), 32 (top, left), 32 (top, right), 32 (bottom, right): © Mark Moffett/Minden Pictures; 9, 10: © iStockphoto; 10 (inset): © Robert Sisson/ National Geographic Stock; 11: © De Agostini Picture Library/Getty Images; 12 (inset): © Satoshi Kuribayashi/Minden Pictures; 13: © Michael & Patricia Fogden/Corbis; 14: © Dong Lin, California Academy of Sciences; 18, 32 (bottom, left): © Mark Moffett/Minden Pictures/National Geographic Stock; 19: © Koshy Johnson/OSF/Photolibrary; 20-21: © Meul/ARCO/Nature Picture Library; 21 (inset): © George Grall/National Geographic/Getty Images; 22: © Ajay Narendra, Australian National University, Canberra; 22-23 (top): © Carlo Bavagnoli/Time Life Pictures/Getty Images; 24 (background): © Piotr Naskrecki/Minden Pictures; 25: © Visuals Unlimited/ Corbis; 26 (inset): © Piotr Naskrecki/Minden Pictures/National Geographic Stock; 28: © Clive Varlack; © John La Gette/Alamy.

Table of Contents

Ants All Around

Do you know how many ants live in the world?

More than

10,000,000,000,000,000.

That's a lot of ants!

Ants live in fields and forests. They live under sidewalks too.

Ants are everywhere!

How do you say
10,000,000,000,000,000?
It's 10 quadrillion!
You say it like this:
kwa drill yun.

An ant is an active insect.

Q What's the biggest kind of ant?

A A giANT

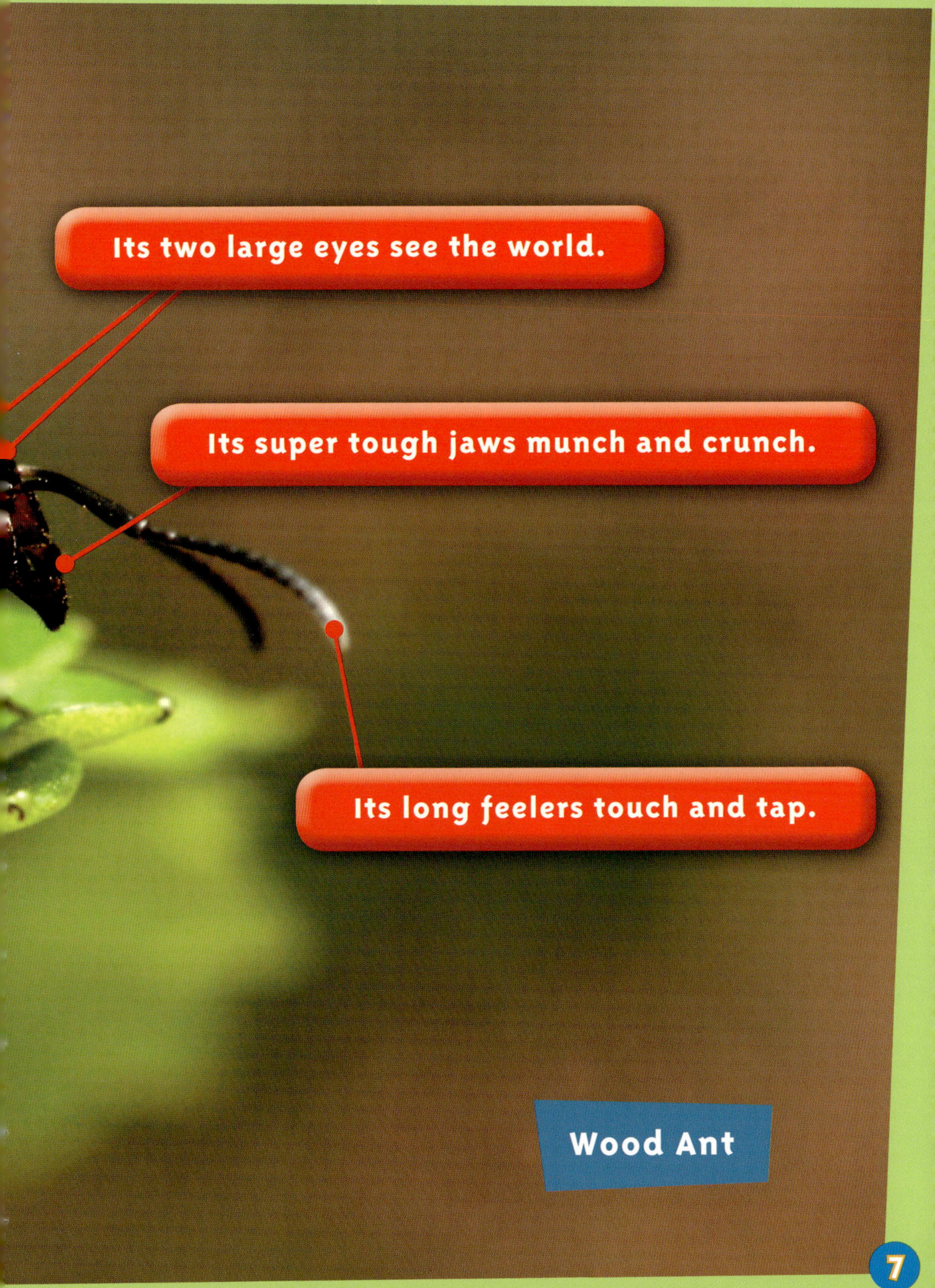

Ants at Home

Army Ant Colony

One ant. Two ants.
Three ants. Four.
See one ant, and you'll
see lots more.

Ants live in large groups.
A group of ants is called
a colony.

WORD BITES

COLONY: A group of ants that lives together. Some colonies have millions of ants.

An ant colony lives in a nest.
Most ants build nests underground.
An ant nest is full of tunnels.
Each tunnel leads to a little room.

Bulldog Ant
inside a tunnel

Underground Ant Nest

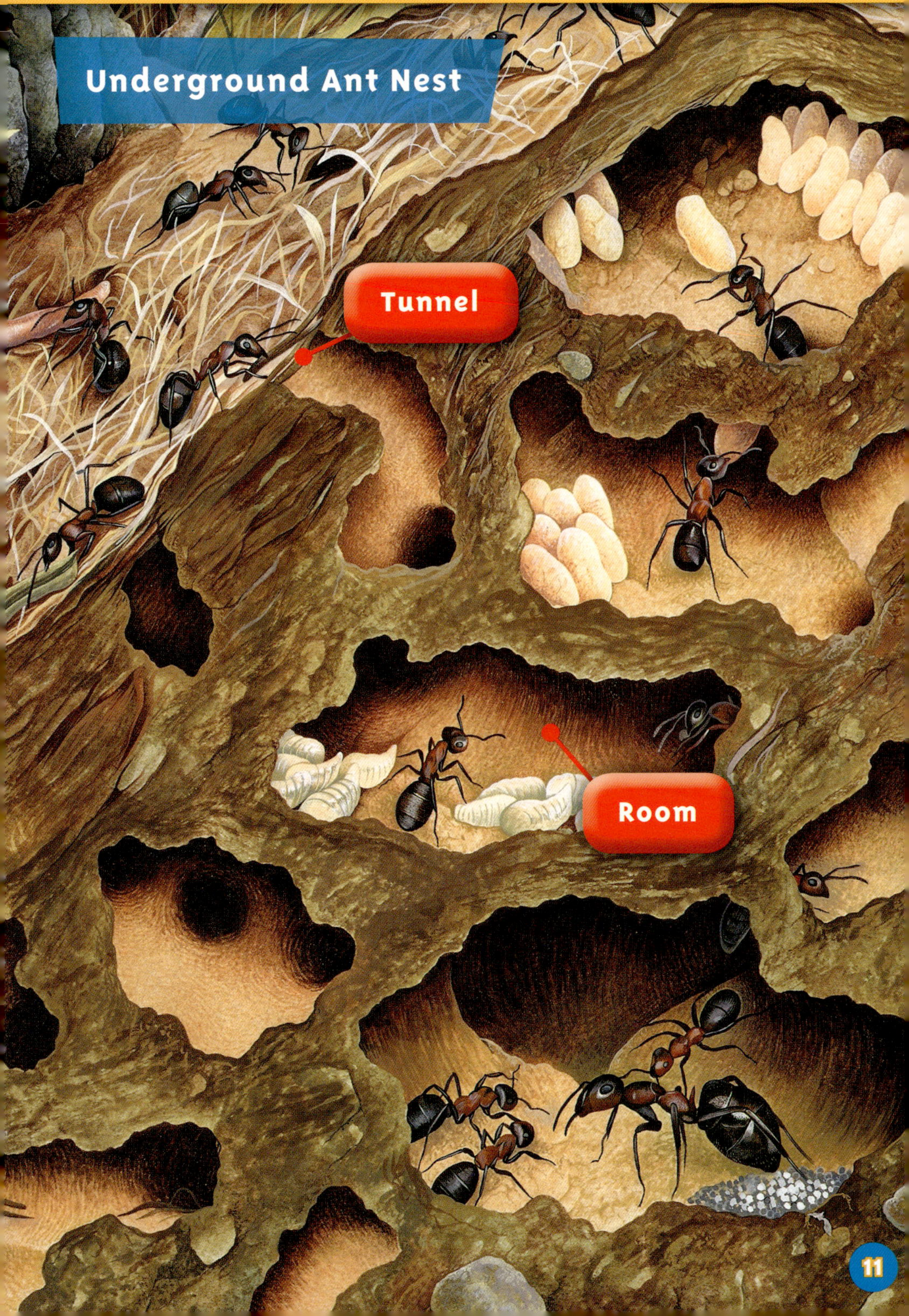

Guinea Ant
nest in a tree

Some ants do not
live underground.

They live…
…inside hollow thorns.
…between rocks.
…in rotting trees.
…in nests made of leaves.

Weaver Ants

The Ant Man

Brian Fisher is a scientist. He looks for new kinds of ants. Some people call him **"The Ant Man."**

Dr. Fisher has found more than 800 new kinds of ants.

He can't wait to find even more!

An Ant's Life

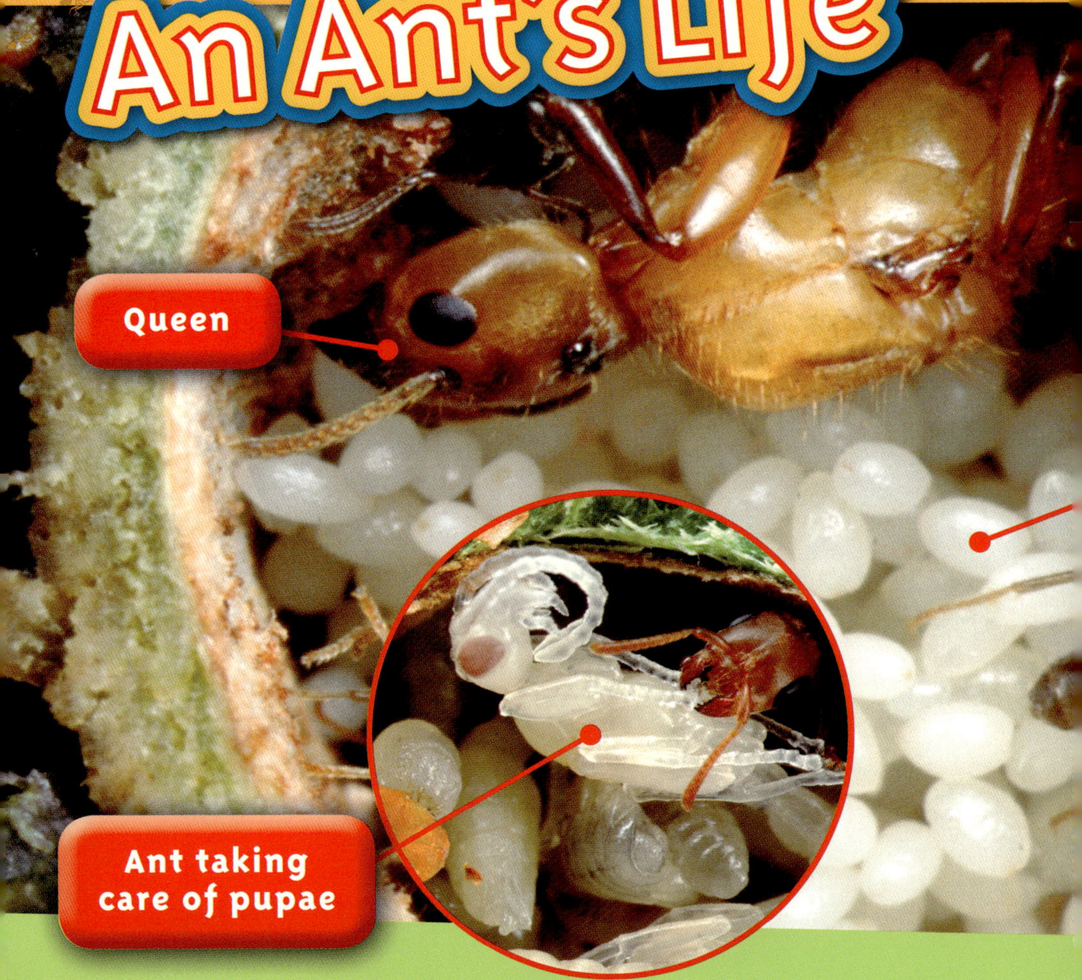

The queen is the biggest ant in a colony. She lays eggs all day long.

When the eggs hatch, little larvae wriggle out. They look like worms.

WORD BITES

LARVAE: The second stage in the life of many insects. Larvae spend most of their time eating and growing.

PUPAE: The third stage in the life of many insects. Some ant pupae are surrounded by a cocoon.

They eat and eat and eat.

Larvae turn into pupae. Pupae do not move. Pupae do not eat. After a few weeks, they turn into adult ants.

Worker Ants

Most of the ants in a colony are workers. All worker ants are female.

Inside the Nest

Some worker ants dig new tunnels. Others take care of eggs, larvae, and pupae.

Outside the Nest

Some worker ants collect food.

Others guard the nest.

Ants with Wings

Garden Ant

Winged Carpenter Ants

A few ants in the colony have wings. Some are females. Some are males.

Ants with wings fly out of the nest. They start new colonies.

Superhero Ants

Aqua Ant

Aqua Ant lives in Australia. She can swim, dive, and even live underwater.

Mama Marvel

Mama Marvel is an African driver ant. She lays fifty million eggs a year.

Hulking Hercules

Hulking Hercules is a bulldog ant. She can lift more than twenty times her body weight.

The Big Biter

The Big Biter is a trap-jaw ant. She has the fastest bite in the animal world. Biter can snap her jaw shut at a speed of 145 miles an hour.

What's for Dinner?

Most ants catch and eat other insects. Some ants eat dead animals. Leafcutter ants grow their own food. They have fungus gardens inside their nest.

Leafcutter Ants and Fungus Garden

Q What did one leafcutter ant say to the other leafcutter ant?

A There's a fungus among us.

WORD BITES

FUNGUS: A living thing that is not a plant or an animal. Mushrooms are a kind of fungus.

Many ants take care of aphids. Aphids are small insects. They make sugary poop that ants like to eat. Mmmm! Yummy!

How do you say aphid? Like this: A fid.

Army ants

Army ants hunt for food every day. The colony looks like a moving, munching carpet.

Army ants sting and bite everything in their path. They can kill insects, spiders, lizards, and baby birds.

An army ant colony can be as wide as a street. It can be longer than a football field.

Fire Ant

Army ants are not the only ants that sting and eat animals.

Fire ants have poison that they inject into other insects, animals, and even people. It leaves a burning feeling. That is how fire ants got their name.

There are more than 280 different kinds of fire ants.

Hooray for Ants!

Ants are an important part of our world. They are food for other animals. Birds, frogs, and spiders eat ants. So do monkeys and aardvarks.

As ants dig tunnels, they mix the dirt. Plants grow better in dirt with ants.

Q Why did the aardvark jump for joy?

A He had ants in his pants.

Leafcutter ants dig up a lot of dirt when they build a nest. Scientists weighed the dirt one colony dug up. The dirt weighed as much as six elephants!

COLONY
A group of ants that lives together

FUNGUS
A living thing that is not a plant or an animal

LARVAE
The second stage in the life of many insects

PUPAE
The third stage in the life of many insects

LEVEL 2

Bats

Elizabeth Carney

NATIONAL GEOGRAPHIC

Washington, D.C.

For Cheri and Raquel, and the
fond memories of our
nighttime mischief.
—E.C.

Published by National Geographic Partners, LLC, Washington, D.C. 20036.

Library of Congress Cataloging-in-Publication Data

Carney, Elizabeth, 1981-
Bats / by Elizabeth Carney.
p. cm.
ISBN 978-1-4263-0710-2 (pbk. : alk. paper) -- ISBN 978-1-4263-0711-9 (library binding : alk. paper)
1. Bats--Juvenile literature. I. Title.
QL737.C5C348 2010
599.4--dc22
2010011636

Cover, Theo Allofs; 1, Martin Withers/ FLPA/ Minden Pictures/ NationalGeographicStock.com; 2, Merlin D. Tuttle, Bat Conservation International; 5, cbimages/ Alamy; 6, Norbert Wu/ Minden Pictures/ NationalGeographicStock.com; 8, Michael Lynch/ Alamy; 9, Carol Farneti Foster/ Getty Images; 10, Tim Laman/ NationalGeographicStock.com; 12, Mark Carwardine/ naturepl.com; 13, Eric Baccega/ naturepl.com; 14, Victor Habbick Visions/ Photo Researchers, Inc.; 16 (top), ImageState/ Alamy; 16 (bottom), Dr. Morley Read/ Shutterstock; 17 (top), Barry Mansell/ naturepl.com; 17 (bottom), Nina Leen/ Time & Life Pictures Creative/ Getty Images; 19, Theo Allofs/ The Image Bank/ Getty Images; 21, Tristan Savatier/ Flickr/ Getty Images; 22, WIN-Initiative/ Getty Images; 23, Dr. Merlin D. Tuttle/ Bat Conservation International/ Photo Researchers, Inc.; 24, Newspix/ Rex USA; 26, Michael & Patricia Fogden/ Minden Pictures/ NationalGeographicStock.com; 28, Ingo Arndt/ Foto Natura/ Minden Pictures/ /NationalGeographicStock.com; 29 (top), Tom Uhlman/ Alamy; 29 (middle), Oxford Scientific/ Photolibrary/ Getty Images; 29 (bottom), Nick Gordon/ ardea.com; 30, Tim Laman/ NationalGeographicStock.com; 30 (inset), Steve Downer/ ardea.com; 31 (top), Konrad Wothe/ Minden Pictures/ NationalGeographicStock.com; 31 (middle), Chris Howes/ Wild Places Photography/ Alamy; 31 (bottom), Hugo Willcox/ Foto Natura Minden Pictures/ NationalGeographicStock.com; 2, (top, left) ; 32 (middle, left), Bob Stefko/ The Image Bank/ Getty Images; 32 (bottom, left), Tim Laman/ NationalGeographicStock.com; 32 (top, right), Victor Habbick Visions/ Photo Researchers, Inc.; 32 (middle, right), Michael & Patricia Fogden/ NationalGeographicStock.com; 32 (bottom, right), Steffen & Alexandra Sailer/ ardea.com.

Table of Contents

What's a Bat?

I sleep by day. I fly by night. I have no feathers to aid my flight. What am I?

The answer is a bat! A bat is a mammal. Mammals are animals that nurse their young, have hair, and are warm-blooded. Humans, dogs, and whales are all mammals. But bats have a special ability. They can fly!

Bat Words

MAMMAL: A warm-blooded animal that drinks its mother's milk, has a backbone, and has hair

Flying fox bats

Bat Food

There are about 1,200 types of bats in the world. Most of them eat insects. Insect-eating bats are usually small in size.

There are more than 150 types of fruit bats. These bats are usually larger and search for sweet fruits and other plants.

Q Why don't bats live alone?

A They prefer to hang out with their friends.

Silky short-tailed bat feeding

A few bats hunt for larger prey, such as frogs, birds, or mice.

Some people think all bats suck your blood. This is not true. Only three kinds of bats drink blood. This group is known as vampire bats. They mostly feed on the blood of animals like cows and deer—not humans.

Vampire bat

Fringed lip bat eating a frog

Night Flight

Did you know that while you're fast asleep, bats are busy filling their bellies? Bats are nocturnal, meaning they're active at night. This way of life has many advantages for a bat. Insect-eating bats often feast

Thousands of wrinkled-lipped bats leaving a cave at dusk

on bugs that come out after dark. Pollen- and nectar-eating bats might feed on plants that only open at night. Nectar is a sweet liquid made by flowers.

Bat Words

NOCTURNAL: The state of being active at night

NECTAR: A sweet liquid made by flowers

Bat Bodies

Scientists call bats Chiroptera (kir-OP-ter-a), a Greek name that means "hand wing." That's because bats have four fingers and a thumb just like us. A thin layer of skin connects the fingers. This forms a wing. Bats also have a sensitive nose and big ears. Their big ears help some bats see with sound!

Q What did the bat say when its buddy asked, "What's up?"

A "The ground."

Bat Words

ECHOLOCATION: A system in some animals for locating objects using sound waves

In the pitch-black night, bats can scoop up a tiny insect with ease. No flashlight required! How do they do it? They make a sound that travels until it hits an object. Then, it bounces off the object and travels back to the bat. From this echo the bat can tell an object's size and how far away it is. This is called echolocation.

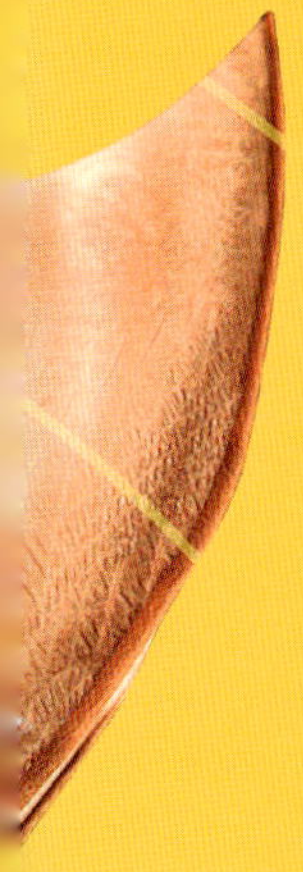

Funny Face

False vampire bat

Amazonian bat

Some bats have strange-looking faces. Special ears, noses, and mouths help bats tune into and make sounds while they use echolocation.

Spotted bat

Big-eared bat

Their faces may look odd to us, but for bats, their features work perfectly!

Hanging Out

When bats are not hunting for food, they're usually hiding in a roost. Roosts can be caves, treetops, or attics. Bats pick places that are well hidden and protect them from bad weather.

When most bats rest in their roost, they hang upside down!

Bat Words

ROOST: The place where animals such as bats and certain types of birds rest

Little redheaded flying foxes roosting in a tree

Have you ever hung upside down in a jungle gym? You might start to feel dizzy. Bats have special veins to keep their blood flowing properly so they never feel dizzy.

Bats can't take off from the ground like birds do. They have to fall into flight. Hanging upside down is the best way to make a quick getaway.

Q Why did the bat get kicked out of the cave?

A Because it had a battitude.

Bats hanging and flying in cave

Baby Bats

Mother and baby bat

Gambian epauletted bat mother and baby flying

Baby bats, called pups, completely depend on their mothers after they're born. They're blind, hairless, and can't fly. They cling to their mother's fur. The pups nurse their mother's milk until their wings are strong enough to fly.

Bat Rescue

During storms in an Australian rain forest, wind can knock baby bats to the forest floor. The babies usually don't survive unless wildlife workers come to the rescue. The lucky bats

Rescued bats in Queensland, Australia

are taken to a bat hospital. The babies are bundled in blankets and fed milk from a bottle. After a few months, they are strong enough to return to the wild.

Nature's Helpers

Hairy-legged nectar bat with pollen on head and shoulders

A world without bats wouldn't be very nice. Bats are an important part of the ecosystem. Insect-eating bats gobble up millions of bugs. Many of these insects are pests that could harm humans or destroy crops. Bats keep their numbers under control.

Other bats keep forests healthy by spreading seeds and pollen. This allows trees and flowers to multiply.

Bat Words

ECOSYSTEM: The environment in which living things live

Bat Myths Busted!

MYTH: Bats are blind.
TRUTH: Bats have excellent eyesight. Some bats hunt using sight alone.

Some people have misunderstandings about bats. Here are a few common myths that drive experts batty.

MYTH: Bats are dirty.
TRUTH: Bats are actually neat freaks. They groom themselves frequently. Mothers lick their babies to keep them clean.

MYTH: Bats get stuck in hair.
TRUTH: With sharp senses and echolocation, bats are very good fliers. They can avoid obstacles the width of a thread.

MYTH: Vampire bats turn into human vampires.
TRUTH: There is no such thing as a human vampire, and bats certainly don't turn into them.

Bat Hall of Fame

TEENIE TINY

The smallest bat in the world is the bumblebee bat. Its wingspan is five inches across. Its body is the size of a jelly bean.

MEGA WINGS

The largest bat is the three-pound flying fox. Its wingspan can be 6 feet long. That's longer than you are tall!

Q Why did the bat use insect repellent?

A Because it was on a diet.

HAPPY CAMPER

The Hondurian white bat makes tents out of leaves to protect itself from constant rain showers.

MOST CROWDED HOME

20 million Mexican free-tailed bats live in one Texas cave. These bats are also the fanciest fliers. They can soar as high as 10,000 feet and zoom through the air at speeds over 40 miles an hour!

BIGGEST APPETITE

Little brown bats can eat up to 1,200 mosquitoes in one night! Yum!

MAMMAL: A warm-blooded animal that nurses its young, has a backbone and hair

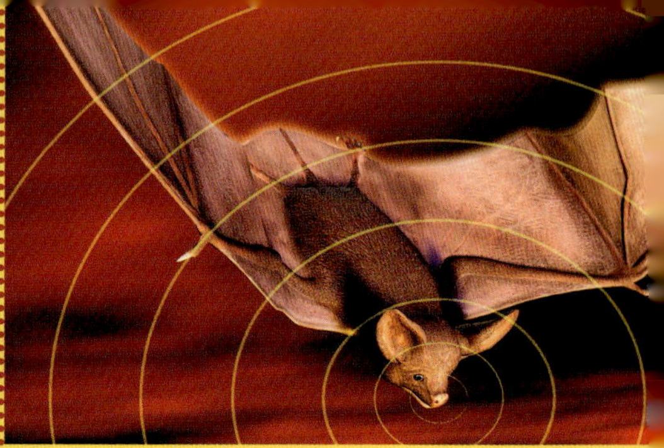

ECHOLOCATION: A system ir some animals for locating objects using sound waves

ROOST: The place where animals such as bats and certain types of birds rest

NECTAR: A sweet liquid made by flowers

NOCTURNAL: The state of being active at night

ECOSYSTEM: The environme in which living things live

LEVEL 2

Snakes

Melissa Stewart

NATIONAL GEOGRAPHIC

Washington, D.C.

For Rubin
—M.S.

Published by National Geographic Partners, LLC, Washington, D.C. 20036

Library of Congress Cataloging-in-Publication Data
Stewart, Melissa.
Snakes / by Melissa Stewart.
p. cm.
ISBN 978-1-4263-0428-6 (pbk. : alk. paper) — ISBN 978-1-4263-0429-3 (hardcover : alk. paper)
1. Snakes—Juvenile literature. I. Title.
QL666.O6S87 2009
597.96—dc22
2008047001

Cover: © Heidi & Hans-Jurgen Koch/drr.net; 1: ©Shutterstock/Skynavin; 2, 20-21, 25 (middle), 32 (bottom, left): © Digital Vision; 4-5: © Michael D. Kern/Nature Picture Library; 6-7: © Jerry Young/Dorling Kindersley/DK Images; 7 (top): © Colin Keates/Dorling Kindersley/Getty Images; 8, 9, 32 (top, right): © Norbert Rosing/National Geographic/Getty Images; 10: © DeAgostini Picture Library/Getty Images; 11 (top): © Joe & Mary Ann McDonald/Getty Images; 11 (bottom, left): © Anthony Bannister/Gallo Images/Getty Images; 11 (bottom, right), 27 (bottom), 32 (middle, left): © Michael & Patricia Fogden/Corbis; 12 (top): © Lowell Georgia/Corbis; 12 (bottom): © Michael & Patricia Fogden/Minden Pictures/National Geographic Stock; 13: © Frank Lane Picture Agency/Corbis; 14 (top), 32 (top, left): © Bianca Lavies/National Geographic/Getty Images; 14-15: © Joe McDonald/Corbis; 16, 25 (top), 32 (bottom, right): © Ashok Captain/ephotocorp/Alamy; 17 (top, left): © Image Source/Corbis; 17 (top, right): © Paul Chesley/Stone/Getty Images; 17 (bottom): © Dwayne Brown/Brownstock Inc./Alamy; 18: © Francois Savigny/Minden Pictures; 18-19 (bottom): © Tony Phelps/Nature Picture Library; 19 (top): © Dr. George Gornacz/Science Photo Library; 19 (bottom, right): © S. Blair Hedges, Ph.D., Penn. State; 22 (top, left): © Frans Lemmens/zefa/Corbis; 22 (top, right), 23 (top, right): © Michael & Patricia Fogden/Minden Pictures; 22-23 (background): © Darrell Gulin/Corbis; 23 (top, left), 31 (top): © Shutterstock; 24: © Dorling Kindersley/Getty Images; 25 (bottom): © Thomas C. Brennan; 26: © Stephen Dalton/Minden Pictures; 27 (top): © Mark Moffett/Minden Pictures/National Geographic Stock; 28, 32 (middle, right): © Theo Allofs/Corbis; 29 (top): © Oliver Strewe/Stone/Getty Images; 29 (bottom): © Werner Bollmann/Photolibrary/Getty Images; 30: © John & Lisa Merrill/Photodisc/Getty Images; 31 (bottom): © A&J Visage/Alamy.

Table of Contents

It's a Snake!

What is long and round,
and slides on the ground?

What can be fat or thin,
and has dry, scaly skin?

AMAZON TREE BOA

What has a tongue that flicks,
and eyes that can't blink?

For goodness sake . . .

. . . it's a snake!

Q What did the hawk order at the ice cream shop?

A *A milk snake.*

A snake is a reptile. Lizards, turtles, and crocodiles are reptiles, too.

All reptiles have tough scales. A snake has stretchy skin between its scales.

A reptile's body is always the same temperature as the air around it. To warm up, a snake lies in the sun. To cool down, a snake moves into the shade.

PYTHON SKELETON

All reptiles have bones inside their bodies. Some snakes have more than 1,000 bones.

This snake has eaten a whole egg. It will crush the egg and spit out the shell.

EGG SNAKE

Snakes All Around

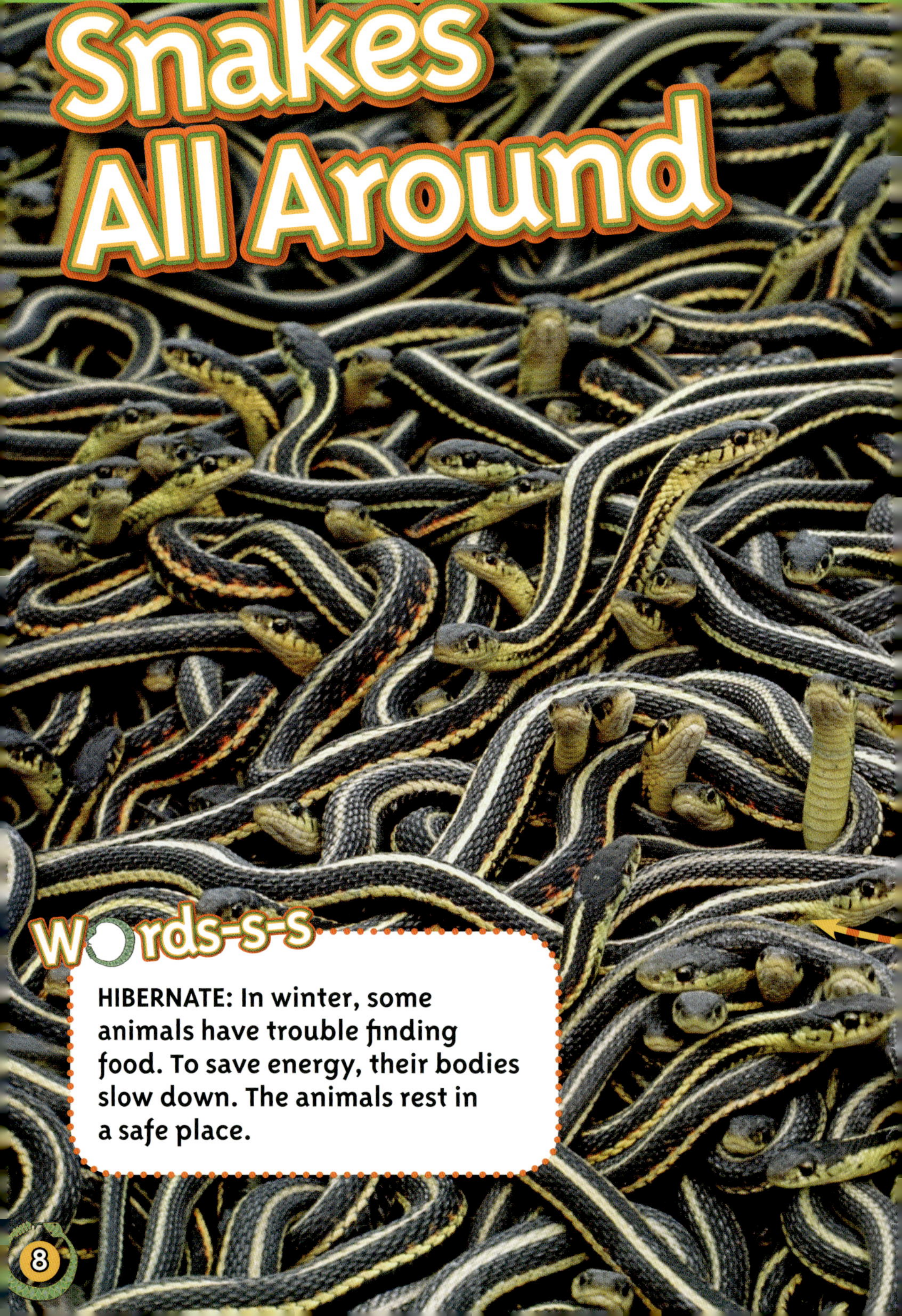

Words-s-s

HIBERNATE: In winter, some animals have trouble finding food. To save energy, their bodies slow down. The animals rest in a safe place.

Snakes live in fields and forests. They live in deserts and oceans too. They even live in city parks. Snakes can live almost anywhere.

Most snakes live in warm places. They stay active all year long.

Some snakes live in cool places. In the winter, they hibernate. Most snakes hibernate alone. Some snakes hibernate in large groups.

Each winter, thousands of garter snakes hibernate together in southern Canada.

In the spring the garters slither out of their warm dens.

Snakes and More Snakes

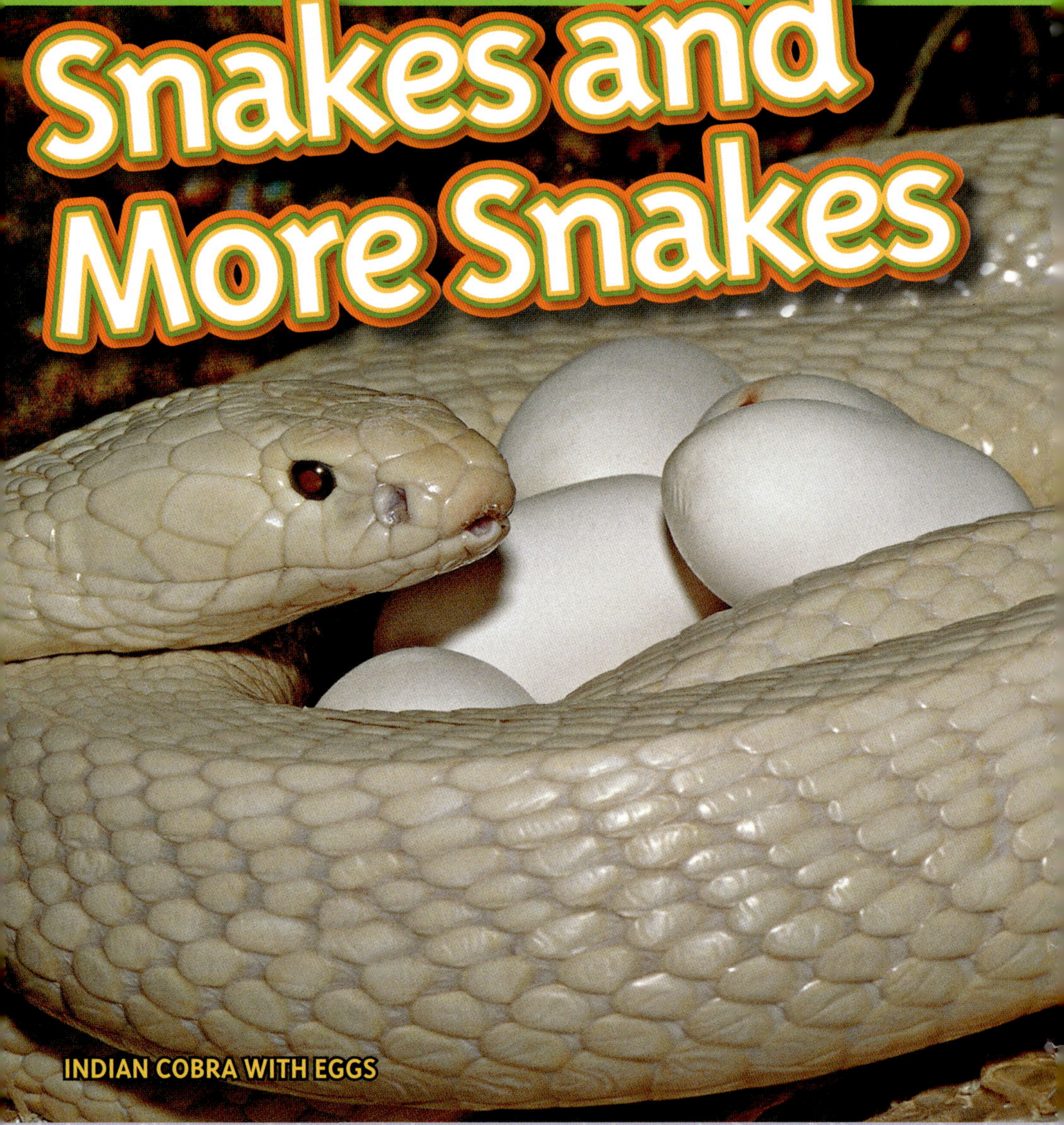

INDIAN COBRA WITH EGGS

In warm places, mother snakes usually lay eggs. Then they slither away. They do not take care of the eggs.

Most snakes lay 20 or 30 eggs. Large pythons may lay up to 100 eggs.

After a few weeks, the eggs hatch. The young snakes look just like their parents.

BURMESE PYTHONS HATCHING

GREEN MAMBA HATCHING

CORAL SNAKE HATCHING

In cool places, snakes usually grow inside their mother's body. A mother snake lies in the sun to keep the little snakes warm.

Q What did the snake do when it didn't get its way?

A *It threw a hissy fit.*

PUFF ADDER WITH SOME OF HER YOUNG

Most mother snakes give birth to between 5 and 20 little snakes. A puff adder can give birth to more than 150 snakes at once. Imagine what it would feel like to have all those tiny wigglers inside your body!

A snake's body never stops growing. Sometimes its skin gets too tight. Then the snake needs to molt.

TIMBER RATTLESNAKE

EGYPTIAN BANDED COBRA

The snake rubs its head against a rock. Its skin splits open. Then the snake crawls forward. Its skin can peel off in one long piece. It's like taking off a sock.

Most snakes molt 3 or 4 times a year.

Words-s-s

MOLT: When animals molt, they lose their old skin, fur, or feathers. New skin is underneath.

On the Move

Most animals have legs and feet. But not a snake. Scutes help a snake move forward.

Words-s-s

SCUTES: The wide scales on the belly of a snake.

PIT VIPER

Q What did the p viper say as it slithered around the rat snake?

A Ex-*scutes*-me.

A python crawls forward in a straight line. Its belly muscles push its scutes against the ground.

Scutes can't grip desert sand. A sidewinding adder has to throw its body sideways to move forward.

PYTHON

SIDEWINDING ADDER

A garter snake curves its body back and forth. Its scutes push against grass and rocks.

GARTER SNAKE

Super Snakes

Heaviest

GREEN ANACONDA
A green anaconda can weigh up to 550 pounds. That's as much as a lion!

There are about 2,700 different kinds of snakes.

Most Poisonous

BEAKED SEA SNAKE
This deadly snake lives in shallow areas of the Indian Ocean. It can stay underwater for up to 5 hours.

Fastest

BLACK MAMBA
A black mamba can travel up to 12 miles per hour. That's twice as fast as most people can run.

Smallest

LESSER ANTILLEAN THREAD SNAKE
The lesser Antillean thread snake was discovered in 2001.

Snake Senses

Snakes use their senses to escape from danger. Senses also help snakes hunt for food.

Snakes with round pupils hunt during the day. Snakes with long, thin pupils hunt at night.

Some snakes smell with their noses. But all snakes smell with their tongues. Their tongues are split at the tip. This helps them know if they should go left or right.

A snake's ears are deep inside its head. Sound travels through a snake's bones to its ears.

Some snakes have heat pits. They can sense the body heat of other animals. Heat pits help snakes hunt at night.

ARUBA RATTLESNAKE

Words-s-s

PUPIL: The dark area at the center of the eye. It lets light into the eye.

Where's the Snake?

GARTER SNAKE IN WATER

Most snakes are hard to see. They blend in with their surroundings.

Can you spot the snakes in these pictures?

Hiding helps snakes stay safe from predators. Hiding also helps snakes catch prey.

Words-s-s

PREDATORS: Animals that eat other animals.

PREY: Animals that are eaten by other animals.

There's the Snake!

Some snakes do not hide from predators. They have other ways of staying safe.

Some snakes play dead when an enemy gets too close.

GRASS SNAKE

Q If a snake went to school, what would its favorite class be?

A *Hiss-tory*

A spitting cobra sprays its predators' eyes with poisonous spit.

A coral snake is full of poison. Its bright colors warn predators to stay away.

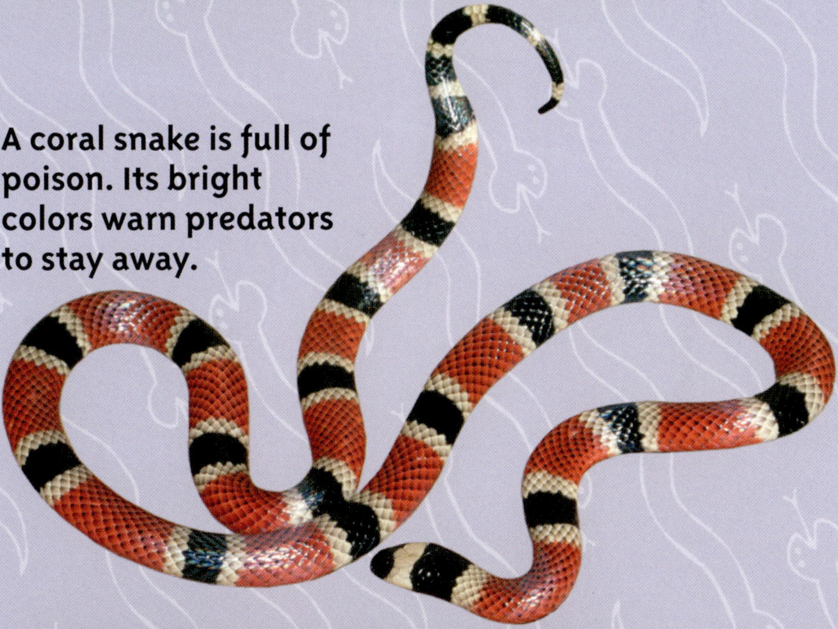

Some snakes hiss at predators. Others rattle their tails. A western hooked-nose snake pushes air out of its back end. The farting sound travels up to six feet.

Snake Snacks

Most snakes eat about 30 meals a year. Snakes catch prey with their sharp teeth.

PUFF ADDER VIPER

Many snakes have more than 200 teeth. If a snake loses a tooth, a new one quickly grows in.

Cobras, vipers, and pit vipers have large teeth. They are called fangs.

TAIWAN HABU VIPER

Poison flows through holes in a snake's fangs. Some poisons stop prey from moving. Other poisons kill the prey.

EYELASH VIPER STRIKING AT HUMMINGBIRD

Q What kind of snake never skips dessert?

A A pie-thon

GREEN TREE SNAKE

Most snakes catch small animals. They eat mice, frogs, fish, and birds. These snakes eat their prey live.

They stretch their mouths wide open. Then they swallow the animal headfirst.

Pythons, boas, and rat snakes can eat large animals. They coil their thick bodies around their prey. Then they squeeze it to death. A large python can easily kill an antelope.

A CARPET SNAKE PUTTING THE SQUEEZE ON A LIZARD

AFRICAN ROCK PYTHON

Snake Pets

Most snakes are not dangerous to humans. Snakes eat mice, rats, and insects that we do not want in our homes or eating our crops. Snakes are an important part of our world.

BOA CONSTRICTOR

Some people like snakes so much that they keep them as pets. Did you know snakes are ticklish? And they are cool and dry and soft. There is nothing else quite like a snake!

BOA CONSTRICTOR

RETICULATED PYTHON

MOLT
When animals molt, they lose their old skin, fur, or feathers. New skin is underneath.

HIBERNATE
Some animals rest during the winter. They slow their bodies down to save energy.

PREDATORS
Animals that eat other animals.

PREY
Animals that are eaten by other animals.

PUPIL
The dark area at the center of the eye. It lets light into the eye.

SCUTES
Scutes are the wide scales on the belly of a snake.